This
Book
Belongs
To _____

Book Club Edition

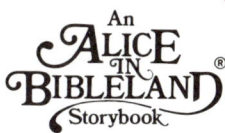

The Story of Esther

Written by Alice Joyce Davidson
Designed by Victoria Marshall

Text copyright © 1989 by Alice Joyce Davidson
Art copyright © 1989 by The C.R. Gibson Company
Published by The C.R. Gibson Company
Norwalk, Connecticut 06856
Printed in the United States of America
All rights reserved

A little girl named Alice
Sat in a cozy nook.
She read about Queen Esther
In her Bible storybook.

And as she read, the airmail bird
Flew to her windowsill
And gave this little note to her
He'd carried in his bill:

"Reading is the special key
To take you where you want to be."

The Bible storybook she held
Became a giant screen.
Alice stepped on through to Bibleland
And came upon this scene.

A Jewish man named Mordecai,
A wise and loyal man,
Was working at the palace
And heard about this plan.

He had a cousin, Esther,
Who was lovely, kind and sweet.
He knew the King would like her
So he arranged for them to meet.

From all the maidens that he met,
The fairest to be seen,
The King chose Esther for his wife
And she became his queen.

Esther made him happy
With her kindness and her charm.
Cousin Mordecai stayed near the gate
And kept the King from harm.

Now, the King was very busy.
His kingdom was quite grand,
So he chose a man named Haman
To help him rule the land.

But Mordecai refused to bow
When Haman passed him by
For the Jews bow down to no one
But God who rules on high.

Then Haman sent out letters
That on a certain date
He'd kill the Jews in Persia
Who'd filled his heart with hate.

Queen Esther went before the King
Dressed in her royal best.
The King asked, "Esther, what's your wish?
I'll give you your request."

But Esther couldn't tell the King,
The time just wasn't right.
"Both of you please come," she said,
"Again tomorrow night."

The King said, "I won't harm you
For you are very dear,
And I won't harm your people
For now everything is clear.

"And just like Esther, we must try
To help each other, too,
And be true to our belief and faith,
And steadfast through and through!"